D1089733

What's the Polish definition of bondage?
(See page 5)

Why do JAPs close their eyes while making love?
(see page 13)

What should a woman dating an Italian have with her at all times?
(see page 26)

How can you tell when a WASP woman is having an orgasm?
(see page 29)

What do you call an African-American homo-sexual?
(see page 38)

What's worse than a dead skunk on your piano?
(see page 60)

Also by Blanche Knott
Published by St. Martin's Press

Blanche Knott's

Truly Tasteless Jokes X

SMP

ST. MARTIN'S PAPERBACKS

TRULY TASTELESS JOKES X

Copyright © 1990 by Blanche Knott.

ISBN: 0-312-92344-9

Printed in the United States of America

St. Martin's Paperbacks edition/November 1990

10 9 8 7 6 5 4 3 2 1

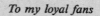

To my loyal fans

CONTENTS

POLISH

How about the three Poles who walked into the restaurant and promptly began jerking off? "I'm sorry, gentlemen," cried the maitre d', rushing over, "but you'll have to leave. We can't tolerate such behavior."

"Then how come there's a sign over there," asked one of the Poles, motioning at the wall, "that says, 'First Come, First Served?'"

•

The six-year-old Polish boy was dying for a tricycle for Christmas. "Does your pecker touch your asshole?" asked his father. When his son shook his head, the father said, "Then you ain't getting a tricycle, kid."

When the kid was twelve he begged his dad for a ten-speed bicycle, but he had to admit that his pecker did not reach his asshole. "So forget about the ten-speed," advised his father.

1

Six years later the kid wanted a new car. "Does your pecker touch your asshole?" asked his father.

"Yup, it does," the boy proudly reported.

"So go fuck yourself."

•

Then there was the Polish mother who decided it was time for her son to learn the great American sport of baseball, so off she went to the sporting-goods store. "How much is this baseball glove?" she asked the salesman.

"Twenty dollars."

"And the bat?"

"Ten dollars."

"I'll take the bat."

"Would you like a ball for the bat?" suggested the salesman hopefully.

"No," answered the mother after thinking it over for a moment, "but I'll blow you for the glove."

•

What's the difference between a Pole and a turd?

The color.

•

Why did the Nazis stop slaughtering the Poles?
    So they wouldn't become an endangered species.

•

Why does it take so long for a Polish baby to be born?
    It's looking for a flashlight.

•

Why did the Polish man lose his job as an elevator operator?
    He couldn't learn the route.

•

Hear about the new Polish invention?
    The solar-powered flashlight.

•

How about the greatest Polish fear?
    Waking up asleep.

•

3

A middle-aged man walked into a store, went up to the counter, and said, "I'd like to order a Polish dog."

Looking up from his ledger, the owner asked, "Are you Polish, by any chance?"

"And just why is that your concern?" retorted the would-be customer. "If I ordered French fries, would you ask me if I were French? I think not. And if I wanted Swiss cheese on my hamburger, would you assume I'm from Switzerland? I doubt it. So why, then, do you ask me if I'm Polish when I order a Polish dog?"

"Because," explained the owner, "this is a florist."

•

How many Poles does it take to rape a girl?

Four. Three to hold her down, and one to read the instructions.

•

Did you hear about the Polish woman who bought an exercise bike and died the very same day?

She tried to ride it home.

•

The eminent Polish physicist was addressing a congress of fellow scientists from around the world. "Gentlemen,"

4

he began, "in the last decade your colleagues in Poland have made miraculous strides towards harnessing the atom. In fact," the physicist went on with evident pride, "we have just succeeded in developing our own prototype of the A-bomb."

A cloud passed over the speaker's face as he admitted that there were still a few wrinkles to work out of the detonating system. "We're using a hammer," he explained, "with a handle fifty miles long . . ."

•

What do you do when a Polish tank is mounting an assault on you?

Shoot the guy pushing it.

•

What's the Polish definition of bondage?

Tying a woman's legs together.

•

Matt Kowalski was walking down the street when he ran into his best friend, Dougie. "Jeez, Matt, what happened to your eye?" asked Dougie, seeing his friend's shiner.

"I went to the eleven o'clock Mass on Sunday," Matt explained, "and when we stood up for the last hymn I noticed that the woman in front of me had a wedgie, so I pulled it out for her."

"Oh," said Dougie.

A week later who should he run into again but Matt, this time sporting two spectacular black eyes. "Matt, you look awful. What happened?" Dougie asked.

Matt hesitated. "See, I went to the eleven o'clock Mass again, and when we stood up to sing the last hymn, my friend Wally noticed that the woman in front of us had a wedgie, so he pulled it out. But I remembered that she didn't like it, so I put it back in for her."

●

How many Poles does it take to milk a cow?

Nine. Four to hold the udders, four to hold the legs, and one to tell them when to move the cow up and down.

●

Know why they don't use the 911 system in Poland?

Because the Poles can't find "11" on their telephones.

●

"Boy, it's hot in here, said the eager girl to her young Polish date, and took off her blouse. The Pole started to moan.

6

"Gee, it's so stuffy," she commented, and took off her pants. The Pole started to cry out loud.

"Gee, I'm just burning up," she cooed, and stripped off her bra and panties. At that, the Pole let out a piercing scream of anguish.

Looking over at him in amazement, the girl asked, "Why the hell are you *crying?*"

"Because my mother told me if I ever saw a naked woman, I'd turn into a rock," gulped the poor fellow between sobs, "and I already feel something hard in my pants."

•

Heard about the Polish chef who wanted to make pineapple upside-down cake?

First he turned over the oven . . .

•

Why did the Pole sit in a tree?

So he could call himself a branch manager.

•

How many Poles does it take to make popcorn?

Four. One to hold the pot, and three to shake the stove.

What's the quickest way to kill a Pole?
  Put him between clean sheets.

Who's the biggest Pole in New York State?
  Stachu of Liberty.

Heard about the signs on garbage trucks in Detroit?
  "We Cater Polish Weddings."

What's a Polish luau?
  A bunch of Poles sitting around a septic tank with straws. . . .

Did you hear about the two Poles who each had a horse and couldn't tell the horses apart? First they put a hat on one, but it fell off. Then they clipped the tail of the other, but that stopped working as soon as the tail grew back. So finally they put the white horse in one stall and the black one in another.

•

What's this? (Put your hand in front of your face and move your head rapidly from side to side.)

A Pole fanning himself.

•

Did you hear about the Pole who took his pregnant wife to the supermarket when she went into labor?

He'd heard they had free delivery.

•

How about the Pole who went to the lumber yard in search of the Draft Board?

•

How about the Pole who wouldn't go out with his wife because she was married?

JEWISH

What's a JAP's idea of perfect sex?
  Simultaneous headaches.

•

What kind of candy did Hitler hate the most?
  Jew-jew beans.

•

A little Jewish guy walked into a bar and was quietly nursing a beer, minding his own business, when a huge hulking fellow came in and sat next to him. All of a sudden the big guy turned and whacked him one, knocking him right off his seat and up against the wall.

Picking himself up and heading back to his barstool,

the little guy turned to the bruiser and asked, "What on earth was that for?"

"That was my karate, from Korea," was the answer.

Figuring him for a nut case, the Jew decided to finish off his beer and get the hell out. But before he could even lift his glass, the big guy turned on him again, this time knocking him clear across the room. Hobbling back to the bar, he asked, "What the hell was that for?"

"That was my judo, from Japan," the big fellow told him smugly.

The Jew realized it was time to go. When he stuck his head in on his way home the next day, the same guy was sitting at the bar. So he went up behind him and— WHAM!—the big man fell to the floor, knocked out cold. To the inquiring bartender the Jew replied, "When that son of a bitch comes to, you can tell him that was my crowbar, from K-Mart."

•

What does a JAP have for breakfast?
    A Tab and a jelly roll.

•

What's the object of a Jewish football game?
    To get the quarter back.

•

An old Jew was retiring from the string and twine business. "Herschel," he implored his best friend, "I got one last load of string. Buy me out so I can retire with an empty shop and a clear heart."

Herschel had no interest in purchasing a load of string but his old friend's impassioned pleading finally wore him down. "Myron, all right, all right," he finally conceded. "I'll buy some of your string—enough to reach from the tip of your nose to the tip of your dick."

To Herschel's surprise, his friend embraced him warmly and left without another word. He was even more surprised when a truck arrived the next morning loaded with a massive roll of string. "Myron, what is this?" he screamed at his friend over the phone.

"My nose is in Palm Beach," explained Myron happily, "but the tip of my dick is buried somewhere outside Minsk."

•

One day the aged Sidney Baumgarden went into St. Anthony's Church and headed straight for the confessional. "Have you anything to confess?" the priest asked gently.

"I do," said the old man. "My wife of fifty-six years, may she rest in peace, passed away two months ago. A week later I met a lovely nineteen-year-old and immediately went to bed with her. I've been sleeping with her ever since. In fact sometimes we do it two or three times a day."

"And how old are you?" queried the priest.

"Eighty-four."

"My God!" blurted the priest. "Go home and say twenty Hail Marys."

"Oh, but I can't. I'm Jewish," Sidney informed him.

"So why in God's name are you telling me all this?" asked the priest.

"I'm telling *everyone!*"

•

Why do JAPs close their eyes while making love?
  So they can pretend they're shopping.

•

How can you spot a disadvantaged Jewish teenager?
  He's driving a domestic car.

AFRICAN-AMERICAN

What do you call one black and six whites?
  An even match.

•

A black man died and started up to heaven. Soon he came across a fork in the road, marked by two signs. Ignoring the one that read "To Purgatory," the man followed the road marked "Straight to Heaven" and pretty soon found himself in front of the pearly gates.

"Hang on, pal," cautioned St. Peter. "You seem pretty confident that you deserve to go straight to heaven. Just what did you do that makes you so special?"

"I married a white woman on the front steps of the courthouse in Mobile, Alabama," replied the man proudly.

"That's pretty special," conceded St. Peter. "When was that?"

"Oh, about five minutes ago."

•

How did the black woman make it into Ripley's Believe-It-Or-Not?

Her snatch was bigger than her husband's lips.

•

What do you call a black on a Japanese motorcycle?

A soot butt on a putt putt.

•

What do you call a black with acne?

Nestles Crunch.

•

A black priest and a white priest happened to die together in a freak car accident. When they arrived at the Pearly Gates, St. Peter looked over his list in some embarrassment and admitted that there must have been a mistake. "Neither of you is due here yet, and God's not in right now," he told them, red-faced, "so I'm not quite sure what to do." Thinking fast, he came up with a proposition: to return them to Earth in whatever form each desired until God returned to clear things up.

"Well, that's fine with me," agreed Father O'Connor. "I'd like to be a butterfly in a great, sunny Alpine meadow."

"Fine," said St. Peter, and Father O'Connor disappeared. "And you?" he asked, turning to the black priest.

"Since I never had the chance, I want to be a stud." And the black priest, Father Johnson, disappeared too.

When God returned the next day, St. Peter filled him in. Nodding, God asked about the priests' whereabouts. "The white one's a butterfly in the Alps," St. Peter told him, "and Father Johnson's on a snow tire in Detroit."

●

How come you never see black people filling out Organ Donor Cards?

Because no one wants to end up with black lung.

●

Two black men were riding around in a limo when Tyrone realized he had to take a wicked shit. "Don' worry about it, man," suggested his buddy. "I'll just pull down this alley, and you stick your butt out the window and let loose."

Two hoboes happened to be sharing a bottle of Ripple just as the limo went by, and Tyrone's turd landed right on one of them. "Jeeesus!" he gasped in shock. "That's the biggest wad of tobacco I've ever seen!"

"No kidding," agreed the other hobo. "Biggest lips, too."

•

What do you call a white man surrounded by three black men?
A victim.

•

What do steroids and the South African government have in common?
They both make blacks run faster.

•

What's a white man feel like when he walks into a Kentucky Fried Chicken?
The filling in an Oreo.

•

What do you call twenty blacks around one white?
The L.A. Lakers.

And twenty whites around one black?
   The Boston Celtics.

•

What has big lips and falls off the Empire State Building?
   Martin Luther Kong, Jr.

•

How come there's never any toilet paper in Kentucky
Fried Chicken bathrooms?
   Cause it's "finger lickin' good!"

•

What's this?

The KKK's idea of a fair fight.

•

A gentleman from Nigeria emigrated to the United States, but it didn't take him long to decide that he didn't really take to his new surroundings. So he saved up all his money, every single penny, and when he went back to the airport to purchase his ticket, he dumped all of the change out on the counter. The ticket agent counted it all up, only to inform him that he was five cents short of the one-way fare.

Desperate, the man went about the airport begging for the nickel he needed to get back to Africa. Finally he approached a white man with his request.

"Five cents!" exclaimed the white guy in disbelief. "If that's all you need, here's a quarter—take four more with you!"

ETHNIC VARIEGATED

When does a Mexican become a Spaniard?
  When he marries into your family.

•

What would Barney and Fred be called if they were black?
  Cocoa Pebbles.

•

What do Chinese people eat for breakfast?
  Rice Krispies, of course.

•

Intelligence sources say that Soviet plans for a memorial to the two workers killed in the Chernobyl disaster have bogged down in arguments as to which two workers it was. . . .

Which brings us to another question: what forty-acre piece of land has only two stones on it?

The Kiev Municipal Cemetery.

•

What did the Soviet nuclear engineer say after the Chernobyl reactor ignited?

"I said 'Bud Light,' Comrade!"

•

How many Ukrainians does it take to screw in a light bulb?

They don't need to; they glow in the dark.

•

Did you hear about the new fast-food chain based in Kiev?

Nuclear Subs. (They're killing off the competition.)

•

21

Did you know that Poland has now installed rural street lighting?

They leave milk cans out by the roadsides.

•

How do you fit 100 Ethiopians in a Volkswagen?
Toss in a piece of bread.

•

How can you fit in one more?
Take out the gearshift.

•

And how do you get them out?
Turn on the air-conditioning.

•

What's Ethiopia's national anthem?
"Stay Hungry."

•

How do you get a female Aggie into an elevator?
  Grease the doorway and throw in a Twinkie.

●

Why did the Aggie drive around the block for five hours?
  His right-turn blinker was on.

●

Hear about the lucky guy who married a woman who was half-French and half-Greek?
  He didn't know which way to turn!

●

What do you call a Filipino contortionist?
  A Manila folder.

●

Why do WASPs play golf?
  It's the only chance they get to dress like pimps.

●

Why were all the Chinese paratroopers killed during practice?

They were using bamboo chutes!

•

What do you call a person who's half-Mexican and half-German?

A Beaner-Schnitzel.

•

Three macho Eskimos were arguing about who had the coldest igloo, so they decided to check each in turn. Sure he'd clinched the argument, the first Eskimo pulled back his polar-bearskin blanket and revealed that his bed was made of ice.

"Nah, mine's colder," claimed the second Eskimo. And when they reached his igloo, it was snowing inside.

"Pretty cold," conceded the third Eskimo, "but I've got you beat." He led the way over to his igloo, where he pulled back the bedcovers to reveal a brown spot on the bed. Chipping it off with an icepick, he tossed it into the fire, and after several minutes a noise came forth like someone passing gas. In response to the puzzled glances of the other two Eskimos, he explained with a smile, "Frozen fart."

•

What do you call a baby Mexican?

A bean sprout.

●

A Russian, a Jamaican, an American, and a Mexican were on a rafting expedition together. Midriver the Russian pulled out a HUGE bottle of Stolychnaya, took a swig, and threw it overboard.

"Hey, what the hell'd you do that for?" blurted the American.

"We have so much vodka in Soviet Union that we can afford to waste it," explained the Russian cheerfully.

A few miles downstream the Jamaican took out a HUGE bag full of marijuana, rolled a giant joint, took a few puffs, and tossed it overboard.

"Jesus, that stuff's expensive," bellowed the American. "What'd you do that for?"

"In Jamaica, ganja grows everywhere, mon," said the Jamaican with a grin. "We can afford to waste it."

Thinking hard, the American settled back into his seat. A few miles downriver he stood up with a smile and threw the Mexican overboard.

●

What do you get when you cross a black with a Japanese?

Someone who on December 7th has an uncontrollable urge to attack Pearl Bailey.

What should a woman dating an Italian have with her at all times?
  The rape hotline number.

•

How many Ethiopians does it take to fix your car?
  None—they don't have good body parts.

•

Why do WASPs fly so much?
  For the food.

•

What do you call an Ethiopian with a swollen toe?
  A golf club.

•

Heard of the famous Chinese philosopher . . .
  Wan Ball Hung Lo?

How many Ethiopians does it take to start a fire?
  None. Why start a fire if there's nothing to cook?

•

What's an Ethiopian sleeping bag?
  A condom.

•

When are the three times a Puerto Rican sees a priest?
  When he's baptized; when he's married; and when he's executed.

•

A man went into the gun store and asked to see the best shotgun available. "Certainly, sir," said the proprietor, rubbing his hands together at the prospect of a big sale. "May I ask just what it is you plan to use the gun for?"
  "Sure, buddy," said the customer. "I want to shoot cans."
  "Did I hear you correctly, sir? You said you want to shoot cans?"

"You heard me fine, buddy," blustered the customer. "Mexicans, Africans, and Republicans."

●

What's a Korean seven-course meal?
  Six puppies and a pound of rice.

●

What does a Puerto Rican kid get for his fourth birthday?
  A switchblade.
For his eighth birthday?
  Laid.
For his tenth birthday?
  Fatherhood.
And for his eighteenth?
  Bail.

●

What do you get when you cross a Caucasian man and a Thai woman?
  Syphilis.

●

What's the ultimate in courage?
  Letting an Ethiopian prostitute give you a blow job.

●

How do you make a Mexican forget how to speak English?
  Offer him a job.

●

How can you tell when a WASP woman is having an orgasm?
  No need; they don't.

●

What's WASP foreplay?
  An engagement ring.

●

What's a Greek gentleman?
  A man who takes a girl out at least three times before he propositions her brother.

Do you know the Korean word for pussy?
  Tung chow.

How about for bad pussy?
  Tung Chow yuk.

Read any of the new Soviet bestsellers?
  The Russian Tragedy, by Whobitsch Yerkokoff
  The Russian Milkman, by I. Sukatitsky and *The Cream of the Russian Army* by Ivan Jackinoff.

One night at three in the morning a Polish man and his wife were awakened by a suspicious noise. Grabbing a flashlight and closely followed by his wife, the Pole headed down the stairs and into the kitchen, where they found a Chinese man eating corned beef out of a can.

  "Will ya get a load of that, Gladys," exclaimed the Pole to his wife. "A Chink in the Armour!"

●

Heard about the Black and the Mexican who opened up a restaurant? It's called Nacho Mama.

●

What do you call white people with big noses?
  Peckerwoods.

●

What do white people's asses and lips have in common?
  They're both flat!

●

A Kentuckian walked into a bar and ordered a bourbon on the rocks. As soon as he was served, he carried the glass into the bathroom and poured the contents down the urinal.

Finally the bartender was unable to contain his curiosity, and asked, "What the hell're you doing?"

"Just cutting out the middleman," he explained.

●

Seen the Canadian bumper sticker?
It says, "I'd Rather Be Driving."

•

What do you call someone who's fifty percent Latino?
Sorta-rican.

•

How many U.S. Marines does it take to screw in a light bulb?
Fifty. One to screw it in and the other forty-nine to guard him.

•

How many Communists does it take to screw in a light bulb?
Two. One to screw it in, and a second to hand out leaflets.

•

How many Jews does it take to screw in a light bulb?

Three. One to call the cleaning lady, and the other two to feel guilty about having to call the cleaning lady.

●

How many Amish does it take to screw in a light bulb?

The Amish don't have light bulbs. They bake pies.

●

How many Irishmen does it take to screw in a light bulb?

Two. One to hold the bulb, and the other to drink till the room spins.

●

And how many Teamsters does it take to change a light bulb?

Ten. You gotta PROBLEM with that?

HOMOSEXUAL

How do you make a fruit punch?
  Goose him.

•

What do gays think of anal sex?
  It hurts at first, but it's fun in the end.

•

What's the most entertaining part about S&M bars?
  The cockfighting in the back room.

•

How can you tell which house the fag lives in?
    On the doormat it says, "Wipe your knees."

•

Why is AIDS like Vitamin C?
    You get both from drinking fruit juice.

•

What happens if you spend the night in a gay bar?
    You'll wake up with a queer taste in your mouth.

•

Why did the Indian chiefs always put their gay warrior at
the head of the battle line?
    Because they're brave suckers.

•

What's AIDS?
    The ultimate diet.

•

How come there's never been a Hurricane Chad?

The U.S. Weather Bureau's waiting for a storm that never stops blowing.

•

If horse racing is the Sport of Kings, what's the Sport of Queens?

Drag racing.

•

What's a lesbian?

A pansy without a stem.

•

What's really selling on Christopher Street these days?

Designer urns.

•

Why did the fag cover himself with whipped cream?

He was going to the costume party as a wet dream.

How come you hear about boys' choirs, not girls' choirs?
Because they sing hymns, not hers.

Why is a fag at an orgy like a turkey?
Because he'll gobble, gobble, gobble till you cut off his head.

Why is heterosexual sperm fresher than homosexual sperm?
Because most gay sperm comes in a can.

Heard about the new gay sitcom?
It's called, "Leave It, It's Beaver."

How come Dukakis got the gay vote?
  Because fags don't like Bush!

●

What's the difference between California and Florida?
  In California, the fruits pick you.

●

Why were all the Greek soldiers wearing black armbands
last month?
  Didn't you hear about the ship that went down with
ten thousand cases of Vaseline?

●

What do you call an African-American homosexual?
  Black and Blew.

●

Why did the preacher get AIDS?
  He forgot to wash his organ between hymns.

A man met an attractive fellow at a gay bar, so he went over to him with an invitation. "Wanna come over to my house and play a game?"

"You bet, big boy," cooed his new friend, so off they went to his apartment, where the first guy explained the rules of the game. "See, I shove something up your butt, and—without looking—you guess what it is." His partner nodded enthusiastically, so he proceeded to insert a broom handle.

"Broom handle!"

"Right. How about this?" And he proceeded to stick a pair of chopsticks up the guy's ass.

"Chopsticks!"

"Right." Next the guy reached for—(at this point the joke teller turns towards his audience and asks, "What's that thing used to unclog toilets and drains?" He continues on until someone in the room says "Plumber's helper" or "plunger," at which point he comments, "Oh —you've played this game before?").

What's the most romantic thing you can say to someone in a gay bar?

"May I move your stool?"

Did you hear about the new hospital for homosexuals under construction outside Atlanta?

It's called "Sick Fags Over Georgia."

•

What was the gay astronomer's favorite come-on?

"Let's go check out Uranus . . ."

•

A regular customer walked into the gay bar and ordered three martinis in a row. "Say, anything wrong?" asked the bartender.

"I've had quite a shock," the man confessed. "I just found out my brother's a queer."

"Could be worse," the bartender pointed out.

"Yeah, maybe . . . but my other brother's gay, too."

The bartender raised his eyebrows. "Doesn't anyone in your family go for women?"

"Yeah . . . my sister."

•

What's the difference between a microwave and anal sex?

Anal sex can brown your meat without cooking it.

If you get malaria from mosquitoes, and sleeping sickness from tsetse flies, how do you get AIDS?
From the asshopper!

•

Why are so many lesbians vegetarians?
They don't want anything to do with meat.

CELEBRITY

What did Donna Rice's father tell her as she was growing up?

"If you're going to abuse a man's job, you'd better learn to use a man's tools."

•

How did Donna Rice explain the fact that she voted Republican?

"Because Bush is in my heart, just like Hart's in my bush."

•

How come Hart decided to re-enter the Presidential race?

Since he likes to eat rice, he figured on picking up the Oriental vote.

So what does "HART" stand for?
  Had Any Rice Today?

What do you call thirteen hookers at a prayer meeting?
  Bakker's dozen.

Did you hear that Jerry Lee Lewis has been chosen by NASA to be the first musician on the new shuttle?
  They want him to sing "Goodness, gracious, great balls of fire!"

How about the new law firm Richard Nixon, Gary Hart, and Ted Kennedy are opening up?
  It's going to be called Trick 'Em, Dick 'Em & Dunk 'Em.

What condition was Christa McAuliffe suffering from?
  Teacher burnout.

●

Know the difference between the Suez Canal and Cindy Lauper?
  The Suez Canal is a busy ditch.

●

There is no—repeat, NO—truth to the rumor that Gary Hart has been messing around with Jim Bakker. After all, there *is* such a thing as separation of Church and State. . . .

●

Richard Nixon gave us Watergate, Ronald Reagan gave us Irangate, and Gary Hart has given us Tailgate.

●

What did Gary Hart scream at Donna Rice?
  "I said, 'Like my erection,' not 'Wreck my election!' "

Did you hear Roseanne Barr was busted coming through customs at JFK?

They looked up her skirt and found 300 pounds of crack!

•

Jimmy Carter, Ted Kennedy, Gary Hart, and Joe Biden were on a campaign trip when their plane ran into a terrible storm. A few minutes later, the pilot announced that the passengers should prepare for a crash landing.

"Save the women," ordered Carter.

"Screw the women," snarled Kennedy.

"Is there time?" asked Hart.

"Is there time?" asked Biden.

•

If Pete Rose got the most base hits, and Hank Aaron got the most home runs, who got hit in the face with the most balls?

Rock Hudson.

•

What did Mrs. Quayle say on her wedding night?
"Dan . . . you're no Jack Kennedy."

•

So what did Lloyd Bentsen say to Kitty Dukakis?
"You're no Joan Kennedy, honey."

•

What do you call three empty whiskey bottles in the corner?
Kitty litter.

•

And what's Kitty Dukakis been doing since Bush got elected?
Drinking 1000 pints of light.

•

What's the difference between Michael Jackson and Richard Pryor?
Richard Pryor got burned by coke, and Michael Jackson got burned by Pepsi.

So how'd they put Jackson's hair out?
  Pryor experience!

●

Know why Jesse Jackson's decided not to run for President again?
  His wife was caught posing for *National Geographic*.

●

How did Karen Carpenter react when she saw the witch melt away in *The Wizard of Oz*?
  "Now *that's* a diet!"

●

Did you hear Jimmy Swaggart's starting up a new magazine?
  It's called *Repenthouse*. And the lead article is "Should the Clergy Do More than Lay People?"

●

What does Dan Rather have in common with reversible panties?
    They both rub Bush the wrong way.

•

Did you hear who just stopped smoking?
    Ted Bundy.

•

What's Ted Bundy's favorite cereal?
    The one that goes, "Snap, Crackle, Pop!"

•

But what's his really, really favorite cereal?
    Crispy Critters.

•

And what's he have with it?
    Extra juice.

•

Know what's his favorite soft drink?
   Jolt.

●

What's black and white and smokes?
   Ted Bundy's new suit.

●

What's Ted Bundy's favorite song?
   "You Light Up My Life."

●

What's the worst kind of light bulb to buy?
   A Bundy Bulb—burn it once and it's dead.

●

How did Ted Bundy pay for his last meal?
   He charged it.

●

What was Bundy's last job?
   Conductor.

•

What did Ted Bundy like most about Florida?
   The heat.

•

What was Ted Bundy's philosophy?
   Everyone should get a charge out of life.

•

How do the citizens of Stark like their Ted Bundy?
   Well done.

•

Why didn't Ted Bundy want to be cremated?
   Because he decided he'd rather be toasted.

•

How did Ted Bundy's mother react when she heard what her son had done?
  She was shocked!

•

And what did she suffer from after his death?
  Sonburn!

•

What's the one thing the crew of the *Challenger* and the engineering staff of NASA have in common?
  They all got fired.

•

What came out of John Lennon's head when he was shot?
  Beatlejuice.

•

What's eighteen inches long and hangs in front of an asshole?
  George Bush's tie.

HANDICAPPED

How do you top a car?
You tep on the gas!

•

A state psychiatrist was touring an insane asylum and was very impressed with its rehabilitative program. In the first room he visited, an inmate was dexterously dribbling a basketball around the small space with astonishing skill, and shooting basket after basket into his wastebasket. "Most impressive, young man," praised the visitor.

"Thanks, doc," said the athlete with a smile. "When I get out of this joint I'm going to be a star with the New York Knicks!"

In the next room the psychiatrist found a patient engrossed by a pitching machine, and he was batting a solid .380. "Not bad," commented the doctor with a smile.

"I'm trying out for the Mets when I get out of here,"

the baseball player said confidently, clearly pleased with his lot.

The scenario in the third room was puzzling, however. Looking through the window, the psychiatrist observed what seemed to be a patient humping a large burlap sack marked "Pecans."

"Good morning, young man," said the doctor, introducing himself. "Can you tell me what you're doing and about your plans for the future?"

"Isn't it obvious, doctor?" asked the inmate, looking up with a wry grin. "I'm fuckin' nuts, and I'm never getting out of here."

●

Heard about the new non-profit institution called AMD?
  It's "Mothers Against Dyslexia."

●

How did Helen Keller's parents punish her?
  By leaving a mouse trap on the edge of the bathtub.

●

How many paranoid schizophrenics does it take to screw in a light bulb?
  Who wants to know?

What do you call a quadriplegic knight who's been out in the rain?

Rusty.

Why didn't the leper cross the road?

He didn't have the balls.

A sailor with a wooden leg, a hook for a hand, and a patch over his eye, walked into a bar and ordered a shot of rum.

"Here you go, buddy, on the house," offered the bartender, being a kind-hearted sort. "Mind if I ask what the hell happened to you?"

"Well, a shark bit off me leg when we capsized off the Azores," recounted the sailor with a weary shrug, "and I lost me hand in a sword fight in Hong Kong, and then I went up on the bridge and a seagull shat in me eye."

"And you lost your eye because of birdshit?" exclaimed the bartender.

"See, I'd only had the hook a week . . ."

What was oral sex to Helen Keller?
   A manicure.

•

Heard about the man who was so mean he went to the local Home for the Blind . . .
   . . . and flattened out all the Braille with a rolling pin?

•

The traveling salesman was delighted when he met an accommodating young woman in the bar of his hotel. He bought her quite a few drinks and a steak dinner, after which she went willingly up to his room. Seeing her start to undress, the salesman followed suit in the bathroom, and was quite astonished when he returned in time to see her unstrapping an artificial leg. By then, however, he was quite drunk and extremely horny, so he went ahead and screwed her.

   The woman fell sound asleep afterwards, but the salesman had never seen an artificial leg up close and was overcome with curiosity. So he started fiddling around, and before he realized what he was doing, it came apart and he couldn't get it back together. Rather panicked, he went down to the lobby in search of some sort of handyman, but all he found was a fellow traveler, reeking of alcohol. Desperate, the salesman approached him and asked for help, stammering, "See, I've got a woman in my room with one leg apart, and I can't get it back to-gether."

"That's nothing," the drunk reassured him. "I've got a woman with two legs apart . . . and I can't find the fucking room."

•

What did one blind Pole keep asking the other blind Pole?

"Is your cock bigger than mine?"

•

How do lepers commit suicide?

By giving head.

•

Hear about the new leper doll?

Wind it up and it falls apart.

•

Why are lepers so obnoxious?

They're always giving you a piece of their minds.

What happened to the leper when he visited Times Square?
    Someone stole his kneecaps.

Why did the boy cut off his father's leg?
    Just once, he wanted to stump him.

How come no upper-echelon corporate executives are lepers?
    They go to pieces under pressure.

Why is this book off-limits to lepers?
    They might laugh their asses off.

Why was the hooker with leprosy hopping around on one foot?

When business got slow, she took twenty percent off.

•

What's the best thing about marrying a nice leper girl?

She can only give you lip once.

•

Why is it a bad idea to date a woman with no hands?

You'll never know how she feels.

•

And now, yet more What Do You Call a Woman With No Arms and No Legs:

—who is surrounded by truckers?

Dinah.

—every four weeks?

Flo.

—with a weak bladder?

Pia.

—with no arms and no legs in a China closet?

Crystal.

—who spreads for bread?

Marge.

—who loves giving blow jobs?
    Heddy.
—who has been forced to eat beans?
    Gail.
—who has no head or torso either?
    Muffy.

•

And What Do You Call a Man With No Arms and No Legs Who:
    —can't get it up?
    Dud.
    —sells drugs?
    Rich.
    —is upside-down in the end zone?
    Spike.
    —has been left out on the lawn all night?
    Dewey.
    —is halfway down Tina Turner's throat?
    Mike.
    —is found in a cracker box?
    Graham.
    —is Spanish, and very pale?
    Juan.
    —is just pretending to have no arms and no legs?
    Josh.
    —is just pretending to have no arms and no legs, for money?
    Con.

ANIMAL

Why do elephants have long toenails?
  To pick their trunks.

•

What's worse than a dead skunk on your piano?
  A diseased beaver on your organ.

•

Jack and Jill went up the hill, riding on a donkey.
  Jill got off to help Jack-off the donkey.

•

What did the cow do after completing her meal at the restaurant?

She chipped the waiter.

•

Two elderly Christian ladies were delighted with a Christmas gift of a beautifully colored parrot. They were less than pleased, however, when the parrot said loudly, "Polly wanna fuck?" just as the parson was sitting down to Sunday dinner.

This sort of language went on for several days, until the ladies felt they had no recourse but to deliver the foul-mouthed bird to a bird reformatory recommended by the parson. All the parrots there had rosaries around their necks and were clinging to Bibles, but the new-comer was undaunted. Settling onto the perch, it squawked, "Polly wanna fuck?"

At this, the oldest, ugliest, meanest, scrawniest parrot threw down her Bible and screamed, "Boys, our prayers have been answered!"

•

What's meaner than a pit bull with AIDS?

The guy who gave it to him.

•

Old Mother Hubbard went to the cupboard
To get her poor dog a bone
But when she bent over
Rover took over
And gave her a bone of his own!

•

If I told you I saw a hole in the ground and in that hole
was a cow and on top of that cow was a cat and on top of
that cat was a rabbit, what would I be telling you?
Holy cow—look at the hare on that pussy!

•

When the Big Bad Wolf hammered on his door and
snarled, "I'm gonna blow yer fuckin' house up," the First
Little Pig was terrified. Squealing in terror, he dashed to
the Second Little Pig's House with the Big Bad Wolf
right on his heels.

The wolf proceeded to bang on the door with all his
might, snarling, "I'm gonna blow your fuckin' house to
smithereens." At this the Second Little Pig jumped right
into his brother's arms in fright. But since the door was
starting to give way under the wolf's pounding, they ran
out the back and made it to the Third Little Pig's House
just ahead of the wolf.

"Yer all pork chops and yer house is history," snarled
the wolf, and started to bash the door in. But just as he
was getting started, a long black limo pulled into the

yard. Three pigs in pinstripe suits got out with machine guns, splattered the wolf all over the front yard, and drove off.

"Wh-wh-who were those guys?" stammered the Second Little Pig, still trembling.

The Third Little Pig explained cheerfully, "Those were the Guinea Pigs."

•

Why does the cat lick her fur?
Because she can't lick her pussy.

•

What do you get when you cross a hawk and a pig?
Ham hawks!

•

How about when you cross a pig with an exotic dancer?
A strip of bacon.

•

Why did the elephant paint his balls red?
  So he could hide in the cherry tree.

So what's the loudest noise in the jungle?
  A giraffe eating cherries.

●

What do you call 1000 rabbits in a row hopping backwards?
  A receding hareline.

●

What did the worm say to the caterpillar?
  "What'd you do to get that fur coat?"

●

A carload of students from an evangelical college in the South were driving down the road when they saw a rabbit get run over by the car in front of them. Unable to think of it suffering for hours, they pulled over next to the poor, half-squished creature and started to pray. They were quite startled when one of the boys pulled a bottle out of his jacket pocket and poured the contents on the rabbit.

Within a minute the animal had visibly perked up, and

in a few more, it got to its feet and took a few experimental hops, stopping to wave at the kids. The bunny hopped over the fence and into the nearby field, then turned and waved again. And then it headed for a nearby grove of trees, stopping once again to turn and wave.

"Holy Smokes, Billy Bob, you mean Holy Water works on animals too?" gasped one of the astonished students.

"Shucks, no," drawled Billy Bob. "That wasn't Holy Water, that was hair restorer with a permanent wave."

•

When the reindeer go out with Santa, where do their wives go?

Downtown to blow a few bucks.

•

What do you get when you cross a porcupine with a tapeworm?

About ten feet of barbed wire.

•

It was the first day of school, and in the fourth grade classroom Miss Hess was having each child describe his or her activities over summer vacation. When it was little Johnny's turn, he was bursting with excitement, and proudly declared, "We shoved firecrackers up pigs' asses!"

"Now Johnny," corrected Miss Hess, "you know we don't say 'ass' here, we say 'rectum'."

"Damned straight we wrecked 'em," cried Johnny. "We blew 'em all to Kingdom Come!"

•

When Al, a New Zealander, met his friend Sid at the local bar, he confessed to having seen the most peculiar thing.

"Oh yeah? What's that?" asked Sid.

"You remember my pals Jim and Mary, right? Well, I just ran into them."

"So?" Sid was getting impatient.

"Well, I just saw Jim screwing a sheep," confided Al.

"You've gotta be kidding!" gasped Sid. "And Mary was there too? What was *she* doing?"

Al leaned close and whispered, "Sid, Mary had a little lamb!"

•

Who's Moby Dick's father?
Papa Boner.

•

Why do dogs stick their noses in women's crotches?
   Because they can.

•

What do you give an obnoxious kid for Christmas?
   A pit bull.

•

Why are dogs better than kids?
   When you get sick of your dog, you can put it to sleep.

•

What did one Hawaiian shark say to the other?
   "Oh, no—not airplane food again."

FEMALE

What's the definition of feminine deodorant spray?
Around-the-cock protection.

•

The hooker was explaining her livelihood to a girlfriend. "I put one stocking on my left leg. Then I put another stocking on my right leg. And between the two . . . I make a living."

•

Forced by bad weather to stop over in a seedy town's only hotel, the businessman decided to put his time to good use. "Do you keep stationery?" he asked the girl at the front desk.

"Yeah," she answered, "until someone touches my clit. Then I go fuckin' crazy."

•

"Honey, I'm home," called Len from the front hall. He was none too pleased when his wife answered, "I'm in the bathroom taking a douche."

"You know I've asked you not to talk like that," Len yelled back.

"Whaddaya want," she called back, "clean talk or clean taste?"

•

Requesting an interview with a loan officer, an inventor explained that he was working on a substance which, applied locally, would make a woman's pussy smell like an orange. The skeptical banker refused the loan.

A year or so later, the banker noticed that the man now had an enormous account. Inviting him in, the banker graciously apologized. "I do hope you don't bear us any hard feelings for turning down your loan request."

"Far from it," replied the inventor cheerfully. "It got me thinking. Instead, I went back to the lab and developed a way to make an orange smell like pussy, and it's been very successful."

•

What did the hooker say when the john handed her the money?

"Thanks—It's been business doing pleasure with you."

•

Glenda was fed up with the stuffy know-it-all seated next to her at the dinner party. "All your hot air doesn't impress me," she finally snapped. "Pick a fight with me and you'd get tit for tat."

"Okay," said the bore cheerfully. "Tat."

•

The salesgirl at the Pink Pussycat boutique didn't bat an eye when the customer purchased an artificial vagina. "What're you going to use it for?" she asked.

"None of your business," answered the customer, beet red and thoroughly offended.

"Calm down, buddy," soothed the salesgirl. "The only reason I'm asking is that if it's food, we don't have to charge you sales tax."

•

The horny guy had just parked the car in Lover's Lane when his girlfriend announced her intention to terminate their relationship. "Aw, honey," he sighed, "how could you do this to me? At least let me look at it once more."

Being a good-natured girl, she obliged, stepping out of the car and pulling up her skirt. It was a moonless night, however, and the boyfriend couldn't see a thing, so he struck a match and bent over for a closer look. "My God," he exclaimed, "can you piss through all that hair?"

"Of course," was the puzzled reply.

"Well you better, because it's on fire!"

•

The waitress had scheduled an appointment after work with her gynecologist, and the doctor was quite taken aback when he came across a tea bag.

"Oh shit," said the waitress when the doctor held it up for her examination. "I wonder what I served my last customer . . ."

•

The first astronaut to land on Mars was delighted to come across a beautiful Martian woman stirring a huge pot over a campfire. "Hi there," he said casually. "What're you doing?"

"Making babies," she explained, looking up with a winsome smile.

Horny after the long space voyage, the astronaut decided to give it a shot. "That's not the way we do it on Earth," he informed her.

"Oh, really?" The Martian woman looked up from her pot with interest. "How do your people do it?"

"Well, it's hard to describe," he conceded, "but I'd be glad to show you."

"Fine," agreed the lovely Martian maiden, and the two proceeded to make love in the glow of the fire. When they were finished, she asked, "So where are the babies?"

"Oh, they don't show up for another nine months," explained the astronaut patiently.

"So why'd you stop stirring?"

•

Definition of henpecked:
A sterile husband afraid to tell his pregnant wife.

•

What do you call a female peacock?
A peacunt.

•

A well-endowed woman entered a chic Madison Avenue boutique and tried on every evening gown in the store. Finally setting eyes on a very sexy, low-cut dress hanging in the display window, she asked the exhausted sales clerk if she could try it on.

"Of course, madam," he muttered through clenched teeth, squeezed into the window, and began the painstaking task of taking the dummy apart to remove the gown. Eventually he succeeded and was able to hand it over to the demanding customer.

"How do I look?" she asked, emerging from the dressing room. "Does it show off my marvelous breasts to advantage?"

"Oh, absolutely," the clerk assured her. "But do hairy chests run in your family?"

•

The manager of a large lumber yard was approached by an elderly blind man looking for employment. "Sorry, pal," he said apologetically, "but you'd have to be able to identify all the different sorts of woods we carry, and frankly with your handicap—"

"No problem, young man, no problem at all," interrupted the blind man cheerfully. "I happen to know a great deal about lumber and my sense of smell is exceedingly keen. Just give me a chance."

Utterly disbelieving, the foreman nonetheless led the old geezer over to a stack of two-by-fours. After a quick sniff, the blind man identified it as pine paneling.

"Right you are," conceded the manager, "but that's an easy one. How about this?" The blind man identified the next piece of wood as oak flooring, the next as birch veneer, then kiln-dried redwood. Flabbergasted, the manager thought of one last test. Instead of a piece of wood, he had his secretary brought out nude and held just beneath the old man's nose. "Well?" he demanded.

"This one's tough," admitted the blind man. "Could you flip it over for me?"

After a few more deep sniffs a big smile broke out on his wrinkled old face. "You tried to put one over on an old blind fellow, but it didn't work," he announced triumphantly. "You can't trick this nose of mine, no sirree. This here piece of wood's the shithouse door off a tuna boat!"

•

How did Helen Keller discover masturbation?
  Trying to read her own lips.

•

So why does she masturbate with just one hand?
  So she can moan with the other.

•

What should a woman give the man who has everything?
  Encouragement.

•

Adam and Eve were strolling in the Garden of Eden after dinner one evening when Eve turned anxiously to her mate. "Adam," she asked, "tell me the truth. Do you love me?"

Adam shrugged. "Who else?"

•

After a few years of marriage the young woman became increasingly dismayed by her diminishing sex life. She tried everything she could think of, from greeting her husband at the door dressed in Saran Wrap to purchasing exotic paraphernalia from a mail-order sex boutique. But none of it had the desired effect on her husband's libido, and finally she persuaded him to consult a hypnotist.

She was delighted that after only a few visits, her husband's ardor was restored to honeymoon dimensions. There was only one annoying side effect: every so often during lovemaking he would jump up and run out of the room for a minute or two. At first his wife didn't want to rock the boat, but eventually her curiosity overcame her better judgment. Following him into the bathroom, she saw him staring into of the mirror, muttering, "She's not my wife. . . . She's not my wife. . . . She's not my wife. . . ."

•

Bert couldn't help noticing that his wife had been increasingly preoccupied and grouchy of late, but he wasn't inclined to do much about it until she leaned across the breakfast table one morning and slapped him hard.

"What the hell's that for?" he shouted, rubbing his cheek.

"That's for being such a lousy lover," she retorted, and stomped off into the kitchen. Bert lost no time in following her over to the sink, where he kicked her so hard she fell on the floor.

"Damn you, you schmuck," she cried. "Why'd you kick me?"

"That," he explained, "is for knowing the difference."

•

As he got into bed the husband was very much in the mood, but was hardly surprised when his wife pushed his hand off her breast. "Lay off, honey. I have a headache."

"Perfect," he responded, without missing a beat. "I was just in the bathroom powdering my dick with aspirin."

•

Little Julie was the apple of her father's eye, especially since she had been born with a heart condition and had always required pampering and special care. When she announced her engagement, Julie's father took it kind of hard, and on the wedding day he took the groom aside for a little talk.

"Listen, I don't know if Julie's told you this," he revealed, "but my little girl's awfully delicate. I think you ought to know that she has acute angina."

"Boy, that's good," said the groom with a grin, "because she sure doesn't have any tits!"

•

How can you find out whether a woman is ticklish?
Give her two test ticles.

•

What are a woman's three greatest lies?
1) You're the best.
2) You're the biggest.
3) It doesn't always smell that way.

•

What do you get when you cross a pyromaniac with a prostitute?
The Burning Bush.

•

If you call a virgin on a waterbed a cherry float, what do you call the same girl on the same bed after she's lost her virginity?

The Red Sea.

•

"Hey, Mick, the usual?" The bartender poured a draft and brought it over to his friend. "What's new?"

"Okay I guess," was Mick's reply. "Sally died, though. Remember her? The widow who lived in the corner house, raised eight kids?" Mick drew on his beer, then said thoughtfully, "Well, at least they're together again."

"Husband and wife, eh?" commiserated the bartender. "That's a nice thought."

"No, no," said Mick brusquely. "Her legs."

•

What's better than a bird in the hand?

A hand in a bush.

•

What do you do at a hooker's birthday party?

Make a wish, and blow.

What chain of food stores do prostitutes patronize?
  Stop 'n' Blow.

If a man with a million dollars is a millionaire, what's a woman with a million dollars?
  Married.

What do women and Tylenol have in common?
  They're dangerous to mess with if someone else has broken the safety seal.

"I've been married three times and I'm still a virgin," complained Myrna to her new friend. "My first husband was a college professor; he only talked about it. My second husband was a doctor; he only looked at it. And my third husband was a gourmet."

Definition of REDUCING SALON:
A place that takes a woman's breadth away.

•

Did you hear about the prostitute who failed her driver's test three times?
She couldn't learn to sit up in a car.

•

What manufacturer leads in vibrator sales?
Genital Electric.

MALE

"Doctor," the man told his physician, "I need a new penis."

The doctor took the request completely in stride. "No problem," he told his patient. "We have a five-incher, a seven-and-a-half-inch model, and a ten-incher. Which do you think would be right for you?"

"The ten-incher," the man decided on the spot. "But would it be possible to take a look at it first?"

"Of course," said the doctor obligingly.

"Gee, Doctor," asked the patient after a few moments, "do you have it in white?"

•

One afternoon the red phone on Prime Minister Thatcher's desk rang.

Gorbachev was on the line, asking an urgent favor. "The AIDS virus has reached the USSR, and we are suffering from an acute condom shortage. In fact," the

Premier confessed, "there are none at all to be had in the Moscow pharmacies. Would it be possible for you to ship me 850,000 condoms—immediately—so that we can deal with this public health threat?"

"Why certainly, Mikhail," replied Mrs. Thatcher gracefully. "Will Friday do?"

"That would be wonderful," sighed the Russian in evident relief. "Oh, and Maggie, one specification: they must be five inches around and nine inches long."

"No problem at all," the Prime Minister assured him breezily. Hanging up, she had her secretary get the largest condom manufacturer in Great Britain on the line, who informed her that a rush order to those specifications would be no problem for his assembly line. "Excellent, excellent," chirped Thatcher. "Now just two more things . . ."

"Yes, Madam?"

"On the condoms must be printed, 'Made in Great Britain,' " Thatcher instructed.

"But of course," the industrialist assured her.

"And 'Medium.' "

●

What's the definition of a bachelor?

A man who prefers to ball without the chain.

●

What's six inches long, has a head on it, and makes women go wild?

Money.

•

(Note: for this joke you need a long-necked beer bottle as a prop.)

A young woman was out on a date and couldn't seem to come up with anything to talk about but her old boyfriend—his hobbies, his car, his habits. (Stroke the length of the bottle lovingly during this part of the joke.)

Finally the new man in her life grew exasperated. "You're always going on about him!" he exploded. "How about thinking about *me* for a change?"

"You've got a point," she admitted. (Move your hand up to stroke just the neck of the bottle.) "I'll try."

•

Little Jack Horner sat in the corner
Fondling his dick and his balls.
Along came his mother,
Who scolded, "Oh, brother—
You better get that off the wall."

•

The newly divorced forty-five-year-old made an appointment with a urologist and told him he wanted to be circumcised. "Most women seem to prefer it," he explained, "and now that I'm dating quite a bit I'd rather not worry about it."

The arrangements were made, and when the patient woke up from the surgery he saw the doctor standing by the bed with a very contrite expression on his face. "I've got good news and bad news," he admitted. "The bad news is that the knife slipped."

"Oh my God," gasped the patient. "What the hell's the good news?"

"It isn't malignant!"

●

After asking the starlet to strip, why did the producer take off his own clothes?

He wanted to see if she could make it big.

●

Why did the tenor hire a hooker?

He wanted someone to hum his parts.

●

What comes after 69?
   Listerine!

•

For Christmas Freddy got the chemistry set he'd been begging for, and he promptly disappeared with it into the basement. Eventually his father came down to see how he was doing, and found Freddy, surrounded by test tubes, pounding away at the wall.

"Son, why're you hammering a nail into the wall?" he asked.

"That's no nail, that's a worm," explained Freddy, and showed his Dad the mixture in which he'd soaked the worm.

"Tell you what, pal," suggested Freddy's father, his eyes lighting up. "Lend me that test tube and I'll buy you a Toyota."

Needless to say, Freddy handed it over, and the next day when he got home from school he spotted a brand-new Mercedes Benz in the driveway. "Hey, Dad, what's up?" he called, running into the house.

"The Toyota's in the garage," explained his father, "and the Mercedes is from your Mom."

•

Why did the football team beat off in the huddle?
   Because the coach had told them to pull themselves together.

Eve and Lola were comparing notes. "I just adore French men," Lola confessed.

"But they're so arrogant and domineering," protested Eve, "and always making jokes at a woman's expense."

"True, all true," admitted Lola with a smile, "but they always eat their words."

•

What do you get when you sleep with a judge?
   Honorable discharge.

•

One day Gary went into the local tattoo parlor with a somewhat odd request. He had this great new girlfriend named Wendy, he explained, and while their sex life was dynamite, he was sure it would be even better if he had her name tattooed on his prick.

The tattoo artist did her best to dissuade him, pointing out that it would be very painful, and that most of the time the tattoo would just read "Wy" anyway. But Gary was undeterred, and went ahead with the tattoo. Sure enough, Wendy was crazy about the tattoo, and their sex grew even wilder and more frequent. Gary was a happy man.

One day he was downtown and had to take a leak in a

public bathroom. At the next urinal was a big black guy, and when Gary looked over he was surprised to see "Wy" on this guy's penis as well. "How about that!" he exclaimed. "Say, is your girlfriend's name Wendy too?"

"Dream on," answered the black guy. "Mine says, 'Welcome to Jamaica and Have a Nice Day.'"

•

A voluptuous blonde was enjoying a stroll around Plato's Retreat, arrogantly examining everyone's equipment before making her choice. In one room she happened upon a scrawny, bald fellow with thick glasses, and to complete the picture, his penis was a puny four inches in length.

Checking it out with a sneer, the blonde snickered, "Just who do you think you're going to please with *that?*"

"Me," he answered, looking up with a grin.

•

A man walked into a bar and started up a conversation with an attractive woman. Pretty soon he confided that he was recently divorced. "My wife and I just weren't sexually compatible," he explained. "I wanted to experiment, you know, try new things, but my wife just wasn't into it. Nice girl, but totally traditional."

The woman's eyes widened as she listened to this tale of marital incompatibility. "That's pretty amazing," she said. "I got divorced a year ago myself, for the same reason. My husband was a total stick-in-the-mud when it came to experimenting sexually." Dropping her voice to a whisper, she confessed to her new acquaintance, "He didn't even like me to be on top."

"Wow, this is *great!*" exclaimed the guy. "You and I are really on the same wavelength. What do you say we go back to my place and get it on?"

"Fine by me," she agreed.

Back at his apartment he issued very specific instructions. "Here's what I want you to do. Take off all your clothes, climb up on my bed, get on your hands and knees, and count to ten."

She obeyed exactly. "Ten," she called out, tingling with excitement. Nothing happened. "Yoo hoo . . . ten," she called sweetly. Then, "I'm waiting. . . ."

"Jeez, I'm sorry," blurted her new acquaintance. "I got off already. I just shat in your purse."

•

Jack was delighted by the opportunity to use the golf course at the swank country club, and even more so when he hit a hole-in-one on the eighth hole. As he bent over to take his ball out of the cup, a genie popped out. "This club is so exclusive that my magical services are available to anyone who hits a hole-in-one on this hole," the genie explained. "Any wish you desire shall be granted."

"How about that!" Jack was thrilled, and immediately requested a longer penis.

"Your wish is granted," intoned the genie solemnly, and disappeared down the hole in a puff of incense.

The golfer went on down the green, and as he walked,

he could feel his dick slowly lengthening. As the game progressed, Jack could feel it growing and growing, down his thigh, out from his shorts leg, down past his knee. "Maybe this wasn't such a great plan after all," muttered Jack to himself, and headed back to the eighth hole with a bucket of balls. Finally he managed a hole-in-one, and when he went to collect the ball, he had to hold up the head of his penis to keep it from dragging on the ground.

Out popped the genie. "This club is so exclusive that my magical services are available to anyone who hits a hole-in-one on this hole. Any wish you—"

"Yeah, yeah, yeah," interrupted Jack. "Could you make my legs longer?"

•

A certain couple loved to compete with each other, comparing their achievements in every aspect of their lives: salaries, athletic abilities, social accomplishments, and so on. Everything was a contest, and the husband sank into a deep depression because he had yet to win a single one. Finally he sought professional counsel, explaining to the shrink that while he wouldn't mind losing once in a while, his unbroken string of defeats had him pretty down.

"Simple enough. All we have to do is devise a game which you can't possibly lose." The shrink thought for a moment, then proposed a pissing contest. "Whoever can pee higher on the wall wins—and how could any woman win?"

Running home, the husband called up, "Darling, I've got a new game!"

"Oooh, I love games," she squealed, running down the stairs. "What is it?"

"C'mon out here," he instructed, pulling her around to the patio. "We're going to stand here, piss on this wall, and whoever makes the highest mark wins."

"What fun! I'll go first." The woman proceeded to lift her dress, then her leg, and pee on the wall about six inches up from the ground. She turned to him expectantly.

"Okay, now it's my turn," said the beleaguered husband eagerly. He unzipped his fly, pulled out his penis, and was just about to pee when his wife interrupted.

"Hang on a sec," she called out. "No hands allowed!"

OLD AGE

Sam wasn't happy about putting his dad in the state nursing home but it was all he could afford—until a lucky investment paid off. The first thing he did with his new-found wealth was to move his father to the best nursing home available.

The old man was astounded by the luxury of his new surroundings. On the first day, he started to list to his right side in front of the television. Instantly a nurse ran over and tactfully straightened him out. Over lunch he started to lean a bit to the left, but within a few seconds a nurse gently pushed him upright again.

That night his son called. "How're you doing Pop?" he asked eagerly.

"Oh Sam, it's a wonderful place," said the father. "I've got my own color TV, the food is cooked by a French chef, the gardens look like Versailles, you wouldn't believe."

"Dad, it sounds perfect."

"There's one problem with the place, though, Sammy," the father whispered. "They won't let you fart."

Ellen and Dan had been married for fifty-seven years when her health began to fail. Eventually she was hospitalized, and within a few weeks it became evident that she had only a few more days to live. "Dan, I have only one last request," she whispered to her husband with the last of her strength.

"Anything, dearest," her husband told her tenderly.

"In all these years we've never had oral sex, and I don't want to die without knowing what it feels like. Go down on me."

Dan was more than a little taken aback, but he figured he'd gotten off easy all those years and that she probably wouldn't last more than another day or two. So he proceeded to close the door and comply with his wife's dying wish. He was even more startled to observe a distinct blush on her cheeks the next day at what he expected would be his final visit. To Dan's amazement and that of the whole hospital, Ellen was sitting up in bed the following day, and within a week she was well enough to be discharged.

Dan was in the room when the doctor told them the happy news, and Ellen was shocked to see her husband break down in tears. "Dan, what's wrong? What's wrong?" she implored.

"I was just realizing," sobbed Dan, "that I coulda saved Eleanor Roosevelt."

An old black man was sitting alone in a restaurant. When the waiter came over he ordered the lemon custard, and when the waiter put it down in front of him, the old man unzipped his pants and proceeded to stick his dick in it.

"What are you doing?" screamed the waiter.

"Ah's old, and ah's tired," explained his customer, "and ah's fuckin' dis custid!"

●

There was once an old woman who owned a dog named Butt and a cat named Pussy. One day her next-door neighbor came by, irate, and complained, "Your damn dog took a shit on my lawn and the next time he does it, I'll pull all the clothes off your clothesline."

Well the dog did it again, and the man pulled the clothes off the clothesline. The dog did it again and the neighbor kicked the dog down the road. At that, the cat went over and scratched up the man's front door, so he shaved the cat's fur off. And that made the old woman so furious that she called the police.

"What seems to be the problem?" asked the cop on duty.

She shrieked, "My neighbor pulled down my pants, shaved my Pussy, and kicked my Butt down the road!"

●

The well-meaning social worker was seeing if Mrs. Englehardt qualified for admission to the local nursing home, and part of the standard procedure was a test for senility. "And what's this?" she asked sweetly of the old German woman, who was sitting at the dinner table.

"Dot? Dot's a spoon," answered Mrs. Englehardt.

"Very good," said the social worker. "And this?"

"Dot's a fork," answered the old woman.

"*Very* good. And this?" asked the social worker, holding up a knife.

"Dot's a phallic symbol."

RELIGIOUS

The Mormon missionaries were explaining their faith to the very proper British matron. "I have three wives," the missionary told her proudly, "and Brother Joseph here has four."

The woman blushed scarlet with shame. "You ought to be—to be *hung!*" she finally stammered.

"You better believe it, lady," said Brother Joseph with a grin.

•

The three nuns had led a completely sinless existence, so when they arrived at the Pearly Gates they were surprised to learn they couldn't enter immediately. "You must first commit a sin, then drink the Holy Water," St. Peter explained gravely.

So the first nun went down to Earth and stole a car. When she came back up, she drank the Holy Water and was admitted to Heaven.

The second nun went down and got laid, came back and drank the Holy Water, and went through the Pearly Gate.

St. Peter turned to the third nun, who was just standing there with a smile on her face. "I've already sinned," she explained. "I peed in the Holy Water."

●

What do you call it when the Pope takes a dump?
Holy Shit!

●

The priest became friends with the rabbi whose synagogue was across the street from his church, and one day he couldn't help remarking on the fact that the church was in perfect repair, while the synagogue needed a new roof and was generally dilapidated. "I don't seem to be able to get a penny out of my congregation," confessed the rabbi, "wealthy though they are. And while your parishioners are mostly blue-collar workers, you're obviously rolling in money."

"I'll show you how I do it," offered the priest generously, and beckoned for the rabbi to follow him into the confession booth.

Soon a penitent entered. "Father, I have sinned," she murmured. "I have committed adultery."

"Three Hail Marys and ten dollars in the collection box," ordered the priest. And so it went; for each of his

96

sinning parishioners, the priest prescribed some Hail Marys and a donation. Eventually the priest turned to the rabbi and suggested that he handle the next one. "Professional courtesy," he said with a smile. "I'm sure you've gotten the point."

So the rabbi was behind the screen when the next person came into the booth. "Father, I committed adultery three times last week," she confessed in a whisper.

"Thirty dollars and nine Hail Marys," ordered the rabbi.

"But Father, I only have twenty-five dollars," she admitted in great distress.

"That's all right," rabbi consoled her, not missing a beat. "Put the twenty-five in the collection box and go home and do it again. We've got a special this week—four for the price of two and a half."

•

What do you get when you cross a nun with a psychopath?

Twisted Sister.

•

What's black, white, and red?

A nun falling down the stairs.

•

So what's black and white?

The priest who pushed her.

•

The Protestant, the Catholic and the Mormon were lunching together at the office cafeteria when the Protestant happily announced that his wife was expecting again. "This'll be our fifth," he pointed out proudly. "Enough for a basketball team."

"Well, I've got ten kids," countered the Catholic, "and my wife's pregnant, too. We're going to have our very own football team."

"I suppose there's something to be said for that," said the Mormon snidely, "but I have seventeen wives. One more, and I've got a golf course!"

•

What did God say when he made the first black minister?

Holy shit!

•

The elderly rabbi and his gorgeous young wife were out taking a stroll one night when a hoodlum jumped out from the shadows, stuck a gun into the rabbi's ribs, and ordered them to hand over their valuables. "Hang on, buddy," he demanded, dragging the protesting woman underneath a street light for a good look. "Not too shabby. Tell ya what—I get a quick screw with the pretty lady and I'll let yous get away safe. Whaddaya say?"

Trying to keep his knees from shaking, the elderly rabbi reached back into his vast memory of Talmudic scholarship and reasoned that the trade would be permissible if their lives were to be spared. He nodded. The hoodlum proceeded to have his way with the rabbi's wife, then vanished into the shadows, and soon the couple was safely back in their apartment.

Needless to say, the young wife was terrified and distraught, and she completely fell apart the next morning when she saw her husband packing his belongings. "Shlomo, don't desert me," she begged, falling to her knees. "You told the man it was all right; you gave your permission."

"The Talmud said it was permissible," the rabbi told her stiffly. "It didn't say you could move."

•

What do you call a fermented apple drink laced with cyanide?

Suicider. (The large size is genocider.)

•

What's the difference between Jim Bakker and Jimmy Swaggart?

Jim Bakker only rips off *half* a million little old ladies a year.

•

Did you hear about the good Catholic girl (boy) who gave up her virginity (his celibacy) for Lent?

•

How about the good Catholic boy who always said Grace before eating out his girlfriend?

•

What do you call it when a girl decides at age sixteen to become a nun?
Premature immaculation!

•

How can you tell the WASP teenager?
He's the kid whose alligator has acne.

•

What do Marines and Catholics have in common?

Anyone who survived parochial school won't have any trouble with boot camp.

•

What do you call 100 Catholics in a Volkswagen?

A family outing.

•

"I gladdened seven hearts today," the priest reported to one of his parishioners with a big smile.

"How's that, Father?"

"I performed three marriages."

"Hmmm," puzzled the parishioner. "I can see that makes six happy people, but . . . ?"

"Listen," explained the priest, "you don't think I do this sort of thing for free, do you?"

MISCELLANEOUS

How many Iraqis does it take to screw in a lightbulb?
Two. One to screw it in and one to screw it up.

•

Why shouldn't the number 288 be mentioned in polite company?
It's two gross.

•

"Yeah, Doc, what's the news?" answered Fred when his doctor called with his test results.

"I have some bad news and some really bad news," admitted the doctor. "The bad news is that you only have twenty-four hours to live."

"Oh my God," gasped Fred, sinking to his knees. "What could be worse news than that?"

"I couldn't get hold of you yesterday."

•

What's the difference between lightning and electricity?

Lightning doesn't cost anything.

•

When should you charge your batteries?

When you don't have enough cash.

•

What do you call a boomerang that doesn't come back?

A stick.

•

What did they yell on an ancient Roman golf course?

"IV!" ("Fore!")

•

What's a toilet's favorite movie?
  Flushdance.

●

The hooker came up to the single man at the bar and said boldly, "I cost three hundred dollars—and I'm worth it."

"Is that so?" asked the fellow, looking her over. "Three hundred bucks is a lot of money."

Snuggling up so that he could smell her perfume and leaning over so he could appreciate her cleavage, the hooker proceeded to elaborate upon the skills, the techniques, the talent and imagination she brought to her trade. "I'll make love to you like you've never been made love to before," she promised with a throaty chuckle. "In fact, whisper any three words—picture your wildest fantasy coming true—and I'll make it happen."

"Any three words? For three hundred dollars?" he asked, perking up considerably.

"That's right, baby," confirmed the prostitute, blowing him a pouty little kiss.

"We've got a deal," cried the new client happily. He pulled her up onto his lap, pulled her long blond hair away from her ear, and whispered, "Paint my house."

●

Why are pool tables green?
  If you had your balls racked, you'd be green too.

What's pink, wet, and smells like pussy?
  My tongue.

•

What do a blow job and Eggs Benedict have in common?
  They're the only two things you never get at home.

•

Coming across a parked car in a dark corner of the camp-grounds, the police officer shone his flashlight in the window. "Yo, you two," he said roughly, "no monkey business. This is a state park."

From within the car came muffled curses, much flailing about, and the protestation, "We were only necking, Officer, honest!"

"Is that so?" asked the policeman. "Well, if I were you, I'd shove your neck back in your pants."

•

Thoroughly fed up with his wife's incessant pissing and moaning, Joe finally agreed to accompany her to a meeting with her therapist. Once there, he made his reluctance quite clear, along with the fact that he had no idea how she found so much to complain about all the time.

"Well, Mr. Johnson," the therapist pointed out gently, "it *is* customary for married people to have sexual intercourse regularly, even frequently. Mrs. Johnson tells me that even on the nights when you don't fall asleep in front of the TV, you never respond in any way to her sexual advances."

"Yeah, well, so?" Joe scratched his head. "So whaddaya recommend?"

"Well, a reasonable minimum might be sexual intercourse at least twice a week," suggested the counselor.

"Twice a week, huh?" grunted Joe, thinking it over. "Okay, I could drop her off on Mondays—but on Fridays she's gotta take the bus."

•

"Hey buddy, can you tell me where hats are sold?" the burly guy asked the information clerk at Macy's. "I've gotta buy one for this big-headed, no-good, son-of-a-bitching son of mine," he explained, and turned to give the little boy at his side such a cuff on the ear that the kid nearly fell over.

Shocked, the information clerk directed him to the fourth floor, where the guy stopped the first salesperson in sight. "I've gotta buy a hat for this big-headed, no-good, little shit son of mine," he told him, kicking the kid in the stomach so hard that he doubled up and keeled over right in the aisle.

"Over there, to the left of the escalator," gasped the salesperson, aghast at the father's brutality.

"I'll be glad to be of service sir," said the salesman when the man reached the hat department, "but first I must ask you why you're beating the child like that."

"Well, I'll tell you," said the burly man, his aggressive demeanor melting away and a dreamy look coming over his face. "See I once made myself a vow that I'd bust my ass, make plenty of money, and marry a beautiful woman with a nice, tight pussy. Well, I made a million dollars by the time I was twenty-five. Then I met this beautiful woman, and she loved me too. Then we got married, and damned if she didn't have the tightest pussy I'd ever felt. And *then* along came this big-headed . . ."

•

What's an unfertilized egg?
    Just another period.

•

When Mike showed up for his appointment with the urologist, the doctor informed him a sperm sample was necessary, and instructed him to go to Room Four. Dutifully going down the hall, Mike opened the door to Room Four and found two absolutely gorgeous women clad in scanty lingerie. They proceeded to arouse him beyond his wildest dreams, and Mike headed back down the hall with a dreamy smile and a *terrific* sperm sample.

Realizing he had to pee, Mike opened the door to the first bathroom he came across, only to interrupt a guy frantically beating off with a copy of *Hustler*. In the second bathroom a fellow was busy masturbating with the company of the *Penthouse* centerfold. Back in the doctor's office and curious as hell, Mike couldn't resist asking the doctor about the other two fellows.

"Oh, those guys?" asked the doctor dismissively. "Those're my Medicaid patients."

●

What did the man in the shower die of?
  Poison Ivory.

●

Visiting New York City for a medical convention, a doctor from the University of Utah took the afternoon off to do some shopping. Wandering into a little antiques store, he came across a curious brass sculpture of a rat and inquired as to the price. "I have to tell you the truth," said the proprietor. "I've sold that piece twice and it's been returned twice—so I'll let you have it for four hundred dollars. It's very old."

The doctor paid and headed out with his purchase in a bag under his arm. Not much later he noticed the shadowy forms of hundreds of live rats scuttling along in the gutters. A little while later the rats had swelled in number to several thousand, and it became evident they were following the doctor. His astonishment turned to disgust and alarm as the rat pack grew to fill up the whole street, so he picked up speed and headed east. When he reached the river, he chucked the brass rat right in, and to his considerable relief the horde of rats followed it to a watery death.

The next morning the doctor was the very first customer in the antiques store.

"No way, buddy, I'm not taking it back a third time," protested the owner.

"Relax, I'm not bringing the rat back," soothed the doctor. "I just wanted to know . . . do you have a brass lawyer?"

●

Why didn't the skeleton cross the road?
He didn't have the guts.

●

This guy saved and saved to buy a motorcycle, and finally came up with enough to buy a handsome, red second-hand Suzuki. "Just one thing, though," cautioned the dealer after pocketing the cash. "You gotta be sure to coat the bike with Vaseline if it starts to rain or it'll rust up on you just about overnight." And he handed him a complimentary jumbo jar of Vaseline.

Happy as a king, the fellow was cruising home when a beautiful girl on a street corner called out. "Nice bike!" Naturally he stopped to talk to her, and a few minutes later she invited him home. "But there's one rule in my house," she warned him. "Whoever says the first word does the dishes."

"Fine by me," he agreed. So the beautiful girl jumped up behind him and directed him to the little house where she lived with her parents. The family rule took on new dimensions when he saw that virtually every surface in the house—tables, chairs, bookcases, counters—was stacked with dirty dishes.

Resolved to shock the others into speaking first, he made love to his new friend right in the middle of the living room floor with both of her parents looking on. Since neither said a word, he turned to the mother, brutally forcing her to submit to his advances right on the kitchen floor. Both father and daughter stood by without saying a word.

At this point a thunderclap shook the house and the first drops of rain began to fall. Remembering his new bike, the guy jumped to his feet and pulled the huge jar of Vaseline out of his pocket. Eyeing the jar and turning visibly pale, the father blurted, "You win, you win!"

•

Jack and Jill went up the hill, each with $1.25. . . .
Jill came down with $2.50.

•

(Note: this one is funnier if you tell it with a lisp.)
Coming into the bar and ordering a double, the man

110

leaned over and confided to the bartender, "I'm *so* pissed off."

"Oh yeah? What happened?" asked the bartender politely.

"See, I met this beautiful woman who invited me back home, and we stripped off our clothes and jumped into bed and were just about to make love when her goddamn husband came in the front door. So I had to jump out the bedroom window and hang from the ledge by my fingernails."

"Gee, that's tough," commiserated the bartender.

"Right, but *that's* not what really got me aggravated," the customer went on. "When her husband came into the room, he said, 'Hey, great, you're naked already—let me just take a leak.' And damned if the lazy son-of-a-bitch didn't piss out the window right onto my head."

"Yecch." The bartender shook his head. "No wonder you're in a lousy mood."

"Yeah, but I haven't told you what *really* got to me. Next I have to listen to them grunting and groaning, and when they're through the husband tosses his condom out the window. And where does it land? My goddamned forehead."

"Jesus, that really is a drag."

"Oh, I'm not finished. See what really pissed me off was when the husband had to take a dump. Turns out the toilet was broken, so he sticks his ass out the window and lets loose right on my head.

The bartender paled. "That would sure mess up my day," he sympathized.

"Yeah, yeah, yeah," the fellow rattled on, "but do you know when I got really, *really* upset? When I looked down and saw my feet were six inches off the ground."

111

What do you sit on that begins with a "d" and ends with a "k"?

A dock.

●

What does N.A.S.A. stand for?

Not A Safe Aircraft. (That's assuming you already heard "Need Another Seven Astronauts".)

●

Two teenage guys are comparing sexual adventures. "Actually, I think Denise has a ticklish pussy," confides Josh.

"Is that so?" asks Roger. "What makes you think so?"

"Well, every time we have sex, she can't stop laughing."

●

"Oh, what a treasure," cooed the new mother in the delivery room.

"Yeah," grunted the new father, taking a closer look. "Let's bury it."

What do the rapist and the conservative have in common?

They both believe in piece through strength.

•

Do you have holes in your socks?

No? How'd you get your feet in?

So how long are your socks?

Two feet.

TOO TASTELESS TO BE INCLUDED

Why do husbands abuse their wives?
  Why not?

•

What's grosser than gross?
  Siamese twins born in '69.

•

What's grosser than gross?
  When a guy gets a boner and runs out of skin.

•

What's grosser than gross?

When you jump off the Empire State Building and catch your eyelid on a nail.

●

What's grosser than gross?

When you throw your dirty underwear against the wall and it sticks.

Even grosser?

When you come back later and find it three feet further up the wall.

●

What's grosser than gross?

When a cheerleader does a split and sticks to the floor.

How do you get her unstuck?

Slide her to the corner.

●

What's grosser than gross?

When you dream about eating pudding and wake up with a spoon in your ass.

●

"Mommy, Mommy, what's an Oedipus complex?"
  "Shut up and kiss me."

•

"Mommy, Mommy where are the marshmallows? Sheldon's on fire."

•

Hopelessly insane, Tom and Dick had been institutionalized for life, but one night they decided to escape from the nuthouse. So they climbed over the fence and hid out in the woods to elude their pursuers. Seven days passed, during which they ate nothing but mushrooms, roots, and berries, which kept them alive but so famished that they began to eye each other hungrily.

On the eighth day Tom was scanning the paper which he'd swiped from the orderly's desk during their escape, and let out a whoop of joy when he hit the Obituary page. It seemed that this guy had been buried in the local cemetery after dying of a heart attack at a ten-course Rotarian banquet. "Don't you get it, Dick?" cried Tom. "The guy *ate* himself to death. He's full of food, and he can't use it anymore, but we sure can."

Dick agreed that it was a great idea, so that night they headed for the cemetery and dug up the corpse. "Damn," cursed Tom, "I forgot to bring a knife. Go see what you can find to cut him open with, okay pal?" But the minute his partner was out of sight, Tom pulled out his pocket knife, sliced the belly open, and began cramming the innards into his mouth as fast as he could. And when Dick came back to the ghastly scene, he was shocked.

"You ghoul!" he screamed. "You animal! You *fiend!* Just look at what you're wolfing down—the guts of a corpse. And a *rotten* corpse at that. As if the stench weren't bad enough, just LOOK at it, the flesh like brown pudding, distended, oozing pus, *SWARMING* with *MAGGOTS.* . . ."

Growing paler and paler during this diatribe, Tom finally barfed up all he'd eaten, right at Dick's feet.

"Aaahh," said Dick with a smile, patting his belly, "nice and WARM. Just the way I like it!"

•

When Jack was born, his mother called out, "What is it, Doctor, a boy or a girl?"

"Got me," admitted the doctor. "I can't get it off the wall."

•

Sister: "You can fuck much better than Daddy does."
Brother: "I know—Mommy told me so."

•

This little old lady and this little old man were taking a walk when they came across a couple screwing on a park bench. "What are they doing?" asked the old woman.

"Making sandwiches," said the old man, and they went on. Soon they walked past two dogs screwing. "What're they doing?" asked the old woman.

"Making sandwiches," explained the old man, and on they went.

A little while later the old woman stopped and took her companion by the elbow. "Say, want to make sandwiches?" she suggested.

"Sure," replied the old man, and they were screwing away when a policeman went by and asked what they were doing.

"Making sandwiches, obviously," retorted the woman. "Can't you see the mayonnaise running down his leg?"

Would you like to see your favorite tasteless jokes in print? If so, send them to:

Blanche Knott
c/o St. Martin's Press
175 Fifth Avenue
New York, NY 10010

We're sorry to say that no compensation or credit can be given. But I *love* hearing from my tasteless readers.

B.K.